Understanding Our Sun

James Bow

CRABTREE
PUBLISHING COMPANY
WWW.CRABTREEBOOKS.COM

Mission: Space Science

Author: James Bow

Editors: Sarah Eason, Tim Cooke, Ellen Rodger

Editorial director: Kathy Middleton

Design: Paul Myerscough, Lynne Lennon

Cover design: Paul Myerscough

Photo research: Rachel Blount

Proofreader and indexer: Nancy Dickmann, Wendy Scavuzzo

Production coordinator and prepress technician: Ken Wright

Print coordinator: Katherine Berti

Consultant: David Hawksett

Produced for Crabtree Publishing by Calcium Creative

Library and Archives Canada Cataloguing in Publication

Bow, James, author
    Understanding our sun / James Bow.

(Mission: space science)
Includes index.
Issued in print and electronic formats.
ISBN 978-0-7787-5395-7 (hardcover).--
ISBN 978-0-7787-5406-0 (softcover).--
ISBN 978-1-4271-2210-0 (HTML)

    1. Sun--Juvenile literature. |
2. Solar energy--Juvenile literature. I. Title.

QB521.5.B675 2019   j523.7   C2018-906110-3
                                           C2018-906111-1

Library of Congress Cataloging-in-Publication Data

Names: Bow, James, author.
Title: Understanding our sun / James Bow.
Description: New York, New York : Crabtree Publishing, [2019] |
  Series: Mission: Space science | Includes index.
Identifiers: LCCN 2018050350 (print) |
  LCCN 2018052349 (ebook) |
  ISBN 9781427122100 (Electronic) |
  ISBN 9780778753957 (hardcover) |
  ISBN 9780778754060 (pbk.)
Subjects: LCSH: Solar energy--Juvenile literature. |
  Sun--Juvenile literature.
Classification: LCC TJ810.3 (ebook) |
  LCC TJ810.3 .B69285 2019 (print) | DDC 523.7--dc23
LC record available at https://lccn.loc.gov/2018050350

Crabtree Publishing Company

www.crabtreebooks.com   1-800-387-7650

Printed in the U.S.A./032019/CG20190118

Published in Canada
Crabtree Publishing
616 Welland Ave.
St. Catharines, Ontario
L2M 5V6

Published in the United States
Crabtree Publishing
PMB 59051
350 Fifth Avenue, 59th Floor
New York, New York 10118

Published in the United Kingdom
Crabtree Publishing
Maritime House
Basin Road North, Hove
BN41 1WR

Published in Australia
Crabtree Publishing
Unit 3 – 5
Currumbin Court
Capalaba QLD 4157

Contents

CHAPTER 1

Our Amazing Sun

Our **Solar System** is our home in the universe. As well as Earth, it comprises seven other planets, dozens of **dwarf planets** and moons, and millions of **asteroids** and **comets** flying around. At the center of everything is the Sun. It makes up 99.8 percent of all the **mass** of our Solar System. Its **gravity** keeps Earth and the other objects in predictable **orbits**, which are regular paths around the Sun. The surface of the Sun is around 9,932 °Fahrenheit (5,500 °C), and its energy gives us light and heat.

At the Center

Our Sun is a star, like one of about 250 billion others in the galaxy. Each star is surrounded by its own solar system of planets and other objects. Along with the Moon, the Sun is one of the easiest **celestial** objects, or objects in the sky, to see from Earth. It is only in the past couple of centuries, however, that people have looked at the Sun in a scientific way. They ask questions about the Sun's physical qualities. How was it created? Why is it so hot? Has it changed? Will it continue to change?

*Earth's **atmosphere** is an envelope of gases that surround the planet. The atmosphere distorts the Sun's light, making it look as though it has rays.*

Scientists darken bright images of the Sun to reveal details of the activity on its surface.

MISSION:
Space Science

Our Sun is 1 astronomical unit (AU) from Earth. An AU is a unit of length used by astronomers to measure distances in space. It is defined as the average distance between Earth and the Sun. This is about 93 million miles (149,668,992 km). At its widest, the diameter of the Sun is about 865,000 miles (1.4 million km). The volume of the Sun is huge—it is so large that 1.3 million Earths could fit inside it.

It is impossible to send spacecraft to the Sun. It is too hot for anything to approach without being destroyed. But by studying the Sun with different scientific instruments, people have come to know a lot about it. We know what it is made of. We know that it is 4.603 billion years old, which is more than 60 million years older than Earth. Many questions still remain, however. Scientists are just beginning to unravel the secrets of the Sun.

New Discoveries

Careful observation and advanced technology reveal new information about the Sun. **Astronomers** are scientists who study space. Using the Hinode spacecraft, they found that the Sun's surface bristles with jets of **X-rays**. These jets fire blobs of energy off the surface at about 1.9 million miles per hour (3.2 million kph). Even after centuries of watching the Sun, our star continues to surprise us.

All life on Earth exists because of the Sun. The Sun gives out energy in the form of light and heat. This energy supports all life on Earth. It warms the oceans and the atmosphere. Green plants convert sunlight into food for themselves and for animals. The Sun's gravity also holds Earth in its regular orbit. If Earth drifted out of its orbit and off into space, the planet would become bitterly cold and all life would end.

The Center of It All

More than 4.6 billion years ago, our Solar System did not yet exist. There was nothing but a cloud of gas and dust. This **interstellar** dust occurs throughout our galaxy.

As gas and dust clumped together at the center of this cloud, it formed a star. As the star attracted more material, its gravity grew stronger. This gravity made the cloud around it spin. More clumps of matter became planets and dwarf planets. They were made from the same materials as the Sun itself.

The Sun generates a huge amount of energy and **magnetism**. Magnetism is a force that attracts or repels other objects. The Sun's magnetism forms the **heliosheath**. This is a **magnetic field** that extends beyond our Solar System. This acts as a shield to protect our Solar System from harmful **cosmic radiation** from deep space.

The Sun's magnetic field may protect our whole Solar System as it orbits the center of the Milky Way Galaxy.

Sun　　Mercury　Venus　Earth　Mars　Jupiter　Saturn　Uranus　Neptune

Dwarfs and Giants

The Sun is a G-type main sequence star, also known as a "yellow dwarf." This is a type of star that is a little more than a million times larger than Earth. More than 70 percent of the Sun is made up of **hydrogen**, which acts as the fuel for the star. Most of the rest is **helium**, with small amounts of other elements. Yellow dwarfs can keep burning their hydrogen for up to 10 billion years.

Many stars in the universe are bigger and burn brighter than yellow dwarfs. These stars, called giants, supergiants, and hypergiants, only last for a few million years before they run out of fuel. Other stars, called red dwarfs, last much longer, but do not burn as brightly. By providing a lot of energy but also burning for billions of years, the Sun may be an ideal star for supporting life on the planets that orbit around it.

Why Study the Sun?

It is difficult to study the Sun. It shines so brightly, it can blind anyone who looks directly at it. Astronomers use special **filters** to protect their eyes from harmful light. They also study the Sun using instruments to detect invisible **radiation**, such as X-rays. This has allowed them to understand a lot more about the Sun. They have figured out that Earth is lucky to be in a part of our Solar System called the **Goldilocks Zone**. This means that Earth is not so far from the Sun that we freeze, and not so close that the Sun makes it too hot for anything to live.

The Power of the Sun

Earth and everyone on it depends on the Sun. It has existed longer than Earth, and it is easy to assume that it will always be there. In fact, the Sun is a huge explosion that has been burning for more than 4.6 billion years. Eventually, it will run out of fuel and die.

Every second, Earth receives enough energy from the Sun to light 17.4 quadrillion lightbulbs (a quadrillion is a 1 followed by 15 zeros). A small backyard receives enough solar energy to power 10 houses for the whole day!

Only about 1 billionth of the energy the Sun releases reaches Earth. The way the Sun releases its energy is inconsistent. **Sunspots**, solar flares, and changes within the Sun can unleash **coronal mass ejections** (CMEs), which are jets of energy. If these **charged particles** hit Earth, they could destroy electricity grids. The power system could be out for years.

A Need to Know

Astronomers observe the Sun closely through special **telescopes** and **solar observatories**, on Earth and in space. Not only does studying the Sun tell us more about the other stars in the sky, but it can also help predict future changes in the Sun's behavior. This might allow us to be better prepared for whatever our nearest star throws at us.

MISSION:
Space Science

The Solar and **Heliospheric** Observatory (SOHO) is a satellite launched in 1995 by the National Aeronautics and Space Agency (NASA) and the European Space Agency (ESA). NASA almost lost the satellite due to problems with its navigation system, but was able to recover the ship. Since then, SOHO has helped scientists observe how the Sun has changed over 20 years, and discovered more than 3,000 comets.

SOHO weighs 1,345 pounds (610 kg). It carries 12 different instruments that look at the Sun in a range of ways.

CHAPTER 2

Looking at the Sun

Today, most scientists believe that our Sun is more than 4.6 billion years old. They believe it formed from a giant, spinning cloud of dust and gas called a solar **nebula**. Gravity pulled the gas and dust together, which made the nebula spin faster. This flattened the nebula into a disk and pulled material toward the center. Eventually, this material grew so big and **dense** that it formed a star. The **atoms** of hydrogen inside were pressed so tightly together they **fused**, or joined, to form helium. This **nuclear fusion** releases huge amounts of energy in many forms, including light and heat.

A solar nebula spins into a disk, encouraging the growth of a star and the formation of planets.

Looking Back in Time

There is plenty of evidence around our Solar System to show how old it is. Using special dating methods, scientists have learned that none of Earth's rocks are more than 4.6 billion years old. Neither are any **meteorites**, which are pieces of rock that fall to Earth from space.

The Sun and the other bodies in our Solar System also have to obey physical laws, which shape how bodies move and **interact**. Scientists are able to test and explore these laws by carrying out experiments, but also by using mathematics, which predicts the orbits of the planets. Mathematicians used computer programs to show how the Sun and the planets interacted with each other over millions of years. That helped them figure out when the planets began moving around the Sun as our Solar System took shape.

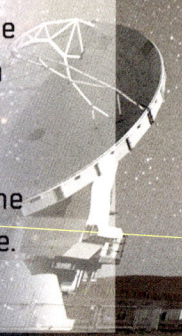

Scientists have also figured out what the Sun is made of, and how much energy it gives out. By calculating how much hydrogen the Sun had as fuel, they discovered how long it would continue to burn.

Looking at the Stars

Astronomers also study stars other than the Sun. Earth's galaxy has around 250 billion stars. Many are the same size as the Sun and burn in a similar fashion. Astronomers use telescopes to study the development of these stars. This shows them how stars are created, and also how they eventually die.

MISSION:
Space Science

The Atacama Large Millimeter Array (ALMA) is a complex containing 66 radio telescopes located in the Atacama Desert near Santiago, Chile. ALMA has taken pictures of HL Tau, a star 450 **light-years** away from Earth. This star is about 1 million years old, and it is surrounded by a solar nebula in which its first planets are starting to form. Discoveries such as this are casting new light on how our Solar System took shape.

The European Union (EU), the United States, Canada, Japan, South Korea, Taiwan, and Chile built ALMA together.

Ancient peoples knew little about the Sun—but they did know it was important to life because it provided light and heat. Many viewed the Sun as a god. Then early astronomers looked closer. They noticed how the Sun's position in the sky changed in a predictable way over the seasons. The Babylonians lived in what is now Iraq, in the Middle East. In the 700s B.C.E., they were among the first people to record **solar eclipses**, when the Moon passes between Earth and the Sun. Babylonian astronomers learned to predict when eclipses could occur again.

The ancient Greeks were the first to observe sunspots. The Greeks believed the Sun was another planet, like Mars and Venus.

New Understanding

Around 270 B.C.E., Greek astronomers suggested that the Sun was at the center of our Solar System, and not Earth. When the Christian religion began, it claimed that Earth was at the center. It was only in the 1500s that the Polish astronomer Nicolaus Copernicus put forward a mathematical model of our Solar System in which the planets orbited the Sun. Other astronomers such as Galileo Galilei used the newly invented telescope to gather evidence to support this model.

In 1687, the English scientist Isaac Newton published calculations based on his theory of gravity. He showed how Copernicus's model could work.

Looking into the Sun

In 1800, British astronomer William Herschel discovered **infrared** radiation from the Sun. Scientists realized the Sun was producing energy they could not see, including infrared and **ultraviolet** radiation, X-rays, and **gamma rays**.

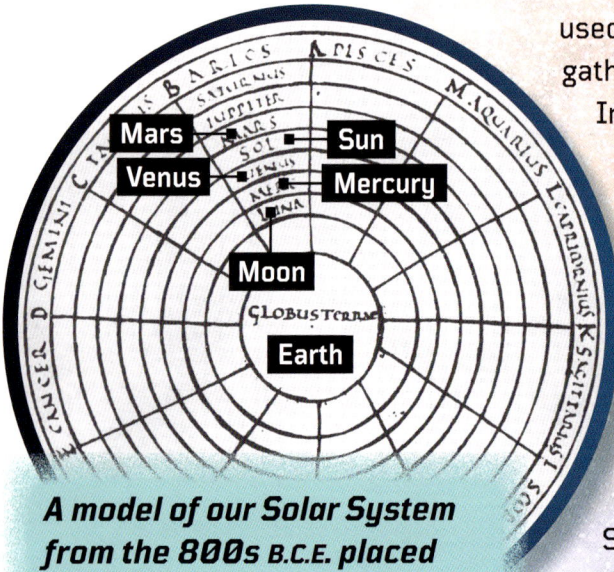

A model of our Solar System from the 800s B.C.E. placed Earth at the center, and the Sun between Venus and Mars.

Astronomer William Herschel studied sunspots.

Scientists use spectroscopy to identify the make-up of distant stars and the planets that orbit them. Such techniques and observations through telescopes allowed scientists to learn how old the Sun was and how it burned. Astronomers were limited to observing the Sun from Earth. But when it became possible to go into space, more mysteries were revealed.

This discovery gave scientists the first clues about what the Sun was made of. When white light passes through a **prism**, which is a triangle of glass, it splits into different colors, like a rainbow. Splitting sunlight, however, reveals dark bands in this rainbow. Scientists discovered that these dark bands are caused when parts of the light are absorbed by different atoms. In the Sun's case, the bands matched where light is absorbed when it hits atoms of hydrogen and helium. This technique is called **spectroscopy**.

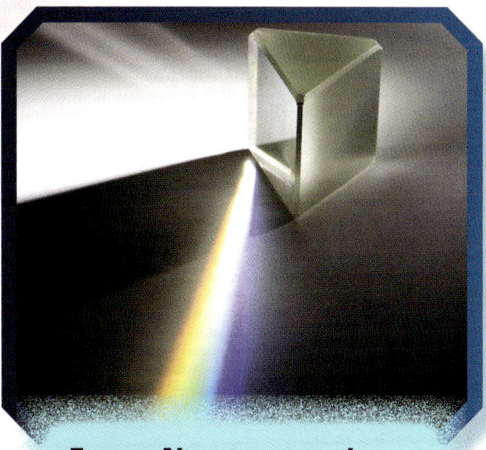

Isaac Newton used a prism to split white light into different colors.

YOUR MISSION

Can you name some of the reasons why scientists are observing the Sun? How might changes in the Sun affect us on Earth? Give reasons for your answers.

For viewers on Earth, the light of the Sun interacts with the atmosphere. This is because Earth's atmosphere acts like a prism and scatters sunlight into a rainbow. The blue and violet colors bend the farthest, while orange and red bend the least. When the Sun is low in the sky, its light has to pass through more of the atmosphere to reach Earth. The air catches the light and scatters it like a prism. The blue, green, and yellow light are bent away from the viewer's eyes, leaving mostly orange and red. This is why sunsets and sunrises often appear red. This effect is heightened if there are particles of **pollution** or dust in the atmosphere. They scatter the light farther. This is known as Rayleigh scattering.

Is the Sun Really Yellow?

At noon, sunlight appears white. Most people, however, think of the Sun as being yellow. It may be that, once the Sun has moved low enough in the sky to look at, its light scatters enough to make it look yellow. The same scattering also explains why the sky looks blue. Blue light bends farther when it is scattered, and fills the sky. Purple light bends even more, so the sky could be purple. However, our eyes are more sensitive to blue light than purple light.

You actually see sunlight a few minutes before the Sun rises or after it sets because the atmosphere bends sunlight over the horizon.

This scattering also causes an effect called the green flash. If conditions are right, such as over a clear horizon like an ocean, the setting or rising Sun can turn green for a couple of seconds. Green flashes are often seen by pilots, especially those flying west toward the Sun, which slows the apparent sunset.

Solar Eclipse

The Moon is responsible for another big event for Sun watchers on Earth: a solar eclipse. This is when the Moon passes between Earth and the Sun at the right distance for the Moon's shadow to fall across a part of Earth. Eclipses alarmed early peoples, who thought they were signs of disaster. However, the Babylonians could accurately predict solar eclipses by 1300 B.C.E. It was not until 1605 C.E. that astronomer Johannes Kepler described why a solar eclipse occurs. Edmond Halley predicted the arrival of a total eclipse on May 3, 1715. He was off by just four minutes.

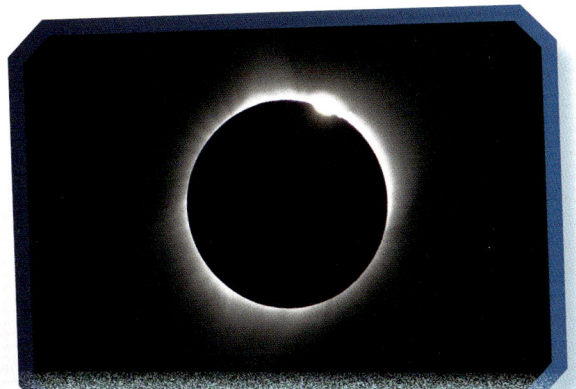

The beads of light seen around the edge of a solar eclipse are the Sun's light shining past the mountains on the Moon.

15

Even though scientists make their discoveries through observation, it is never safe to look directly at the Sun. Even just after a solar eclipse, the light from the Sun is so bright that it can damage people's eyes. Sunlight is so intense that **lenses** can focus it into a beam that burns things and damages equipment. Astronomers observe the Sun using special filters to block most of its light. Cameras can also snap pictures very quickly, so they capture just a fraction of a second of light on film. Unlike regular telescopes, large solar telescopes have to compensate for the Sun's heat. The heat can cause movement in the air, which changes the image. Solar observatories are usually located in towers and painted white to keep things cool. Solar telescopes were placed atop high mountains to avoid the atmosphere bending the light.

Scientists use filters to take pictures of the Sun, both to reduce its brightness and as a shield against invisible infrared and ultraviolet light.

Solar Discoveries

Solar observations from Earth were enough to show that the Sun was not a simple disk of light. Astronomers could see sunspots and solar features such as flares on its surface. By studying these features, astronomers figured out that the star takes 24.47 Earth days to rotate at its **equator**, or widest section, but up to 38 days at its **poles**.

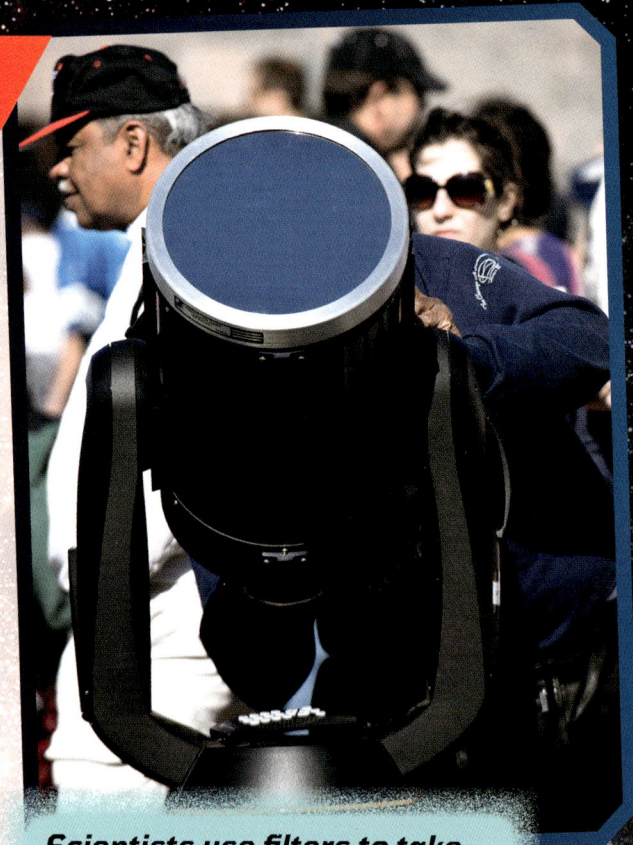

As technology improved, astronomers made more discoveries. In 1942, radar signals were jammed due to radio waves from a large solar flare. Today, astronomers use radio telescopes to monitor solar flares. The way these sound and radio waves pass through the Sun also tells scientists a lot about what is going on inside the Sun, where hydrogen is turned into helium.

Telescopes in Space

To get even better views of the Sun, astronomers have had to go to space. Skylab was a space station that included a solar observatory. It orbited Earth between 1973 and 1979. Skylab took more than 150,000 photographs of the Sun, including X-ray and ultraviolet images. It recorded spectacular solar flares rising from the Sun's surface. In 2008, the Fermi Gamma-ray Space Telescope began orbiting Earth and measured gamma rays put out by the Sun. This type of radiation is more energetic than light or even X-rays. In 2012, the telescope detected a solar eruption that produced gamma rays with 2 billion times the energy of visible light.

SIZE OF EARTH

Scientists inserted an image of Earth into this picture to show its size relative to the Sun.

MISSION:
Space Science

The Daniel K. Inouye Solar Telescope is being built in Hawaii. It is expected to get its first views of the Sun in 2019. The observatory is located 1.8 miles (3 km) above sea level. There are already a number of telescopes in Hawaii. They are built on tall mountains in the middle of the Pacific Ocean. This gives clear images by reducing distortion from the atmosphere and pollution.

Ships to the Sun

Astronomers would like to send space **probes** with instruments to gather information from the Sun. Missions to the Sun are rare, however, because the Sun's heat makes them very difficult. Between 1965 and 1968, Pioneers 6, 7, 8, and 9 orbited the Sun at distances as close as 0.75 AU—a bit farther out than Venus. These were the first probes to measure the Sun's magnetic field and its **solar wind**. The solar wind is a stream of particles released from the Sun's corona, or upper atmosphere. Between 2011 and 2015, NASA's MESSENGER probe orbited Mercury, with an orbit that kept it on the **night side** for long periods of time to allow the probe to cool from the Sun's heat. It got within 0.30 AU of the Sun, and measured the energy of solar flares.

Parker Space Probe

In August 2018, NASA launched the Parker Solar Probe. It was the first mission designed to fly into the Sun's corona, orbiting 3.8 million miles (6.2 million km) above the surface. Astronomers hoped the mission would answer questions about why the Sun's corona is much hotter than its surface.

heat shield

The Parker Solar Probe has a heat shield 4.5 inches (11.5 cm) thick to protect its instruments.

Lagrange Points

In 2018, ESA revealed plans for a new solar mission. If it receives approval, this mission will launch four probes from Earth in the 2020s. These probes would orbit the Sun at two special points in Earth's orbit around the Sun where the gravity of Earth and the gravity of the Sun are perfectly balanced. These positions are called Lagrange points. Similar positions exist between any two bodies in space where one orbits the other.

The Sun's X-rays and gamma rays are specially colored in this image to make them visible.

Earth has five Lagrange points, which are known as L1 to L5. The mission is planned to visit two of them. These are L1, directly between Earth and the Sun, and L5, which follows Earth's orbit, but is 45 degrees away. The probes would measure the speed of the solar wind, observe the Sun's corona, and look for solar flares and coronal mass ejections that may be heading from the Sun toward Earth.

YOUR MISSION

What activities take place on the Sun's surface that could damage probes trying to find out more about the Sun? What measures have scientists taken when building space probes to help protect them from the Sun's heat and activities?

CHAPTER 3

Inside the Sun

The surface of the Sun is around 9,941 °Fahrenheit (5,505 °C), but the core is many times hotter. The high temperatures are caused by the intense pressure of the Sun's gravity. The pressure in the core is enough to **compress**, or press together, hydrogen atoms so they join to form helium. The Sun consumes more than 600 million tons (544 million mt) of hydrogen every second and has been doing this for over 4.6 billion years. This process of nuclear fusion releases great amounts of energy. The energy spreads out from the core, off the Sun's surface, and into space.

Hot Center

The core of the Sun extends from the center of the star to around one-quarter of the way to the Sun's surface. It is in this region that the Sun generates most of the energy that eventually reaches Earth in the form of light. Although the Sun is mostly made of hydrogen, helium is a heavier atom that is pulled toward the center of the star. Most of the helium produced by fusion is found in the core. Helium makes up 75 percent of the mass of the Sun's core.

The Sun is built up of a series of layers. The core alone is 2.5 times the size of the giant gas planet Jupiter.

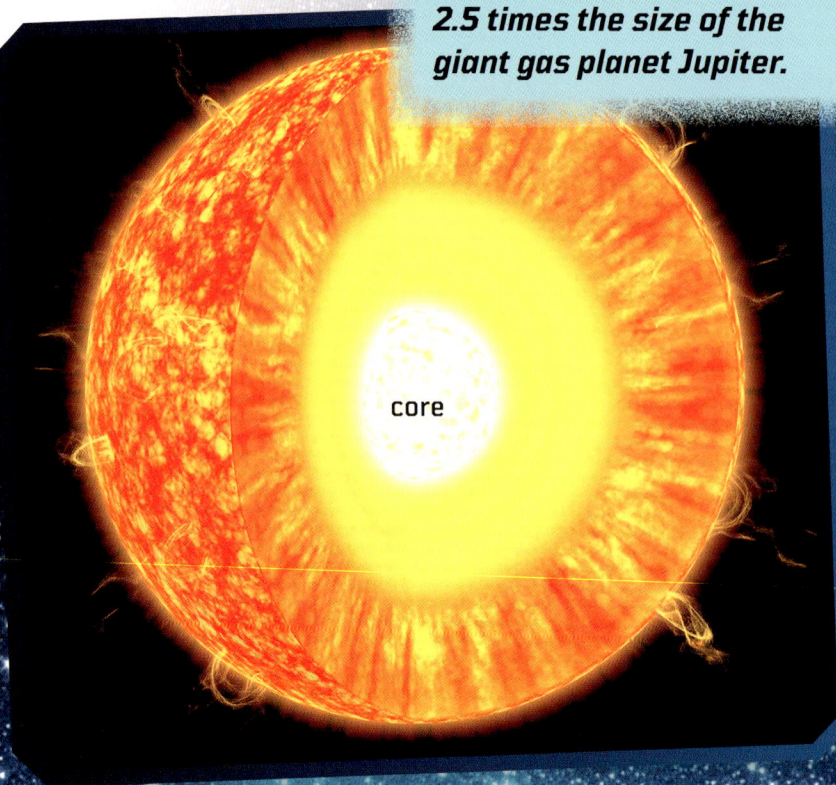

core

Squashed Energy

Although it is made of hydrogen and helium, which both occur naturally as gases, the Sun itself is not actually a ball of gas. Instead it is a form of matter called a **plasma**. Familiar types of plasma in everyday life we notice on Earth are lightning and neon signs.

Plasma is a high-energy state of matter. It is possible to use energy in the form of heat to alter materials, such as by boiling liquids so that they turn into gases, such as steam. In the same way, the energy in plasma breaks the bonds between atoms and their **electrons**. Electrons are tiny particles that are contained within atoms. They carry an electric charge and are what electricity is made of. An electrical current is created by a stream of charged electrons. The core of the Sun is under so much pressure from gravity that the plasma and other materials are 150 times denser than liquid water.

MISSION:
Space Science

At the Max Planck Institute for Plasma Physics in Germany, scientists are trying to recreate the Sun's core conditions. This kind of nuclear fusion could be a clean and limitless source of energy for Earth in the future. Heating hydrogen atoms to 144 million °Fahrenheit (80 million °C), scientists will push them together with lasers, fusing them to helium and releasing energy. They will use magnets to keep the atoms from touching anything else.

Outside the core, the Sun changes. Nuclear fusion no longer happens. The band from 20 percent to 74 percent of the way to the Sun's surface is known as the **radiative zone**. Matter is so dense in the radiative zone that the **photons**, or light particles, produced by the Sun's core only travel a short distance before they hit another particle and are either absorbed or scattered. It takes 171,000 years for energy from the core to leave the radiative zone. The temperature ranges from 27 million °Fahrenheit (15 million °C) near the core to 2.7 million °Fahrenheit (1.5 million °C) near the surface of the Sun.

A Hot Layer Cake

At the top of the radiative zone is the tachocline. This is a region between the inner layers of the Sun and the outer third. Above the tachocline is the **convective zone**. This zone is a place where the Sun moves like a fluid, rotating slowly at the poles and more quickly at the equator. The difference in rotation speeds between the convective zone and the radiative zone generates **electromagnetic energy**. This turns the Sun into a powerhouse that generates a huge magnetic field.

The convective zone takes up most of the outer 30 percent of the Sun, except for a thin layer at the surface.

Sunspots are dark, cooler patches that move around on the surface of the Sun.

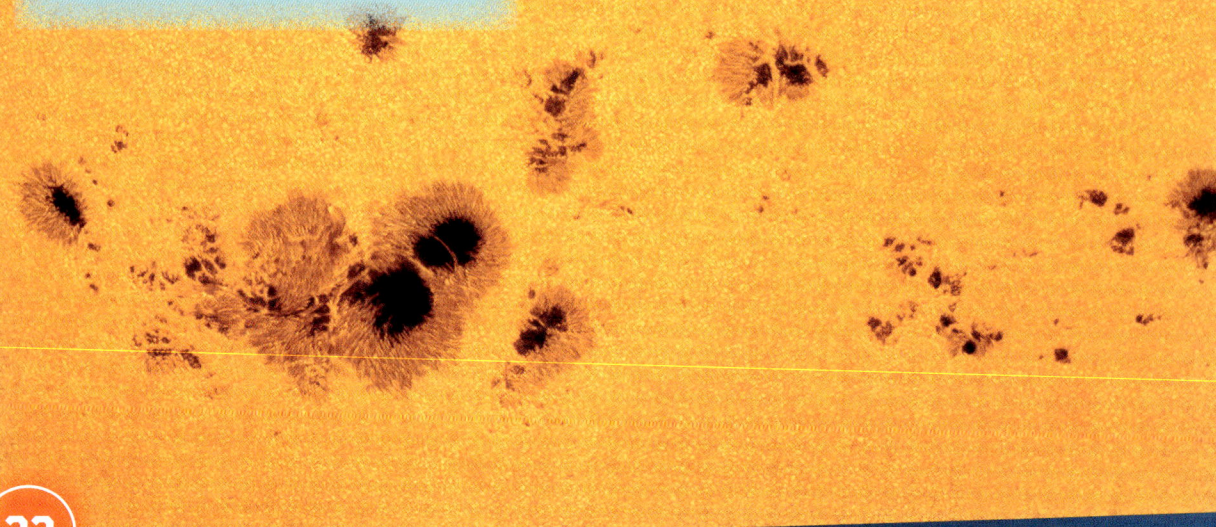

sunspot

solar flare

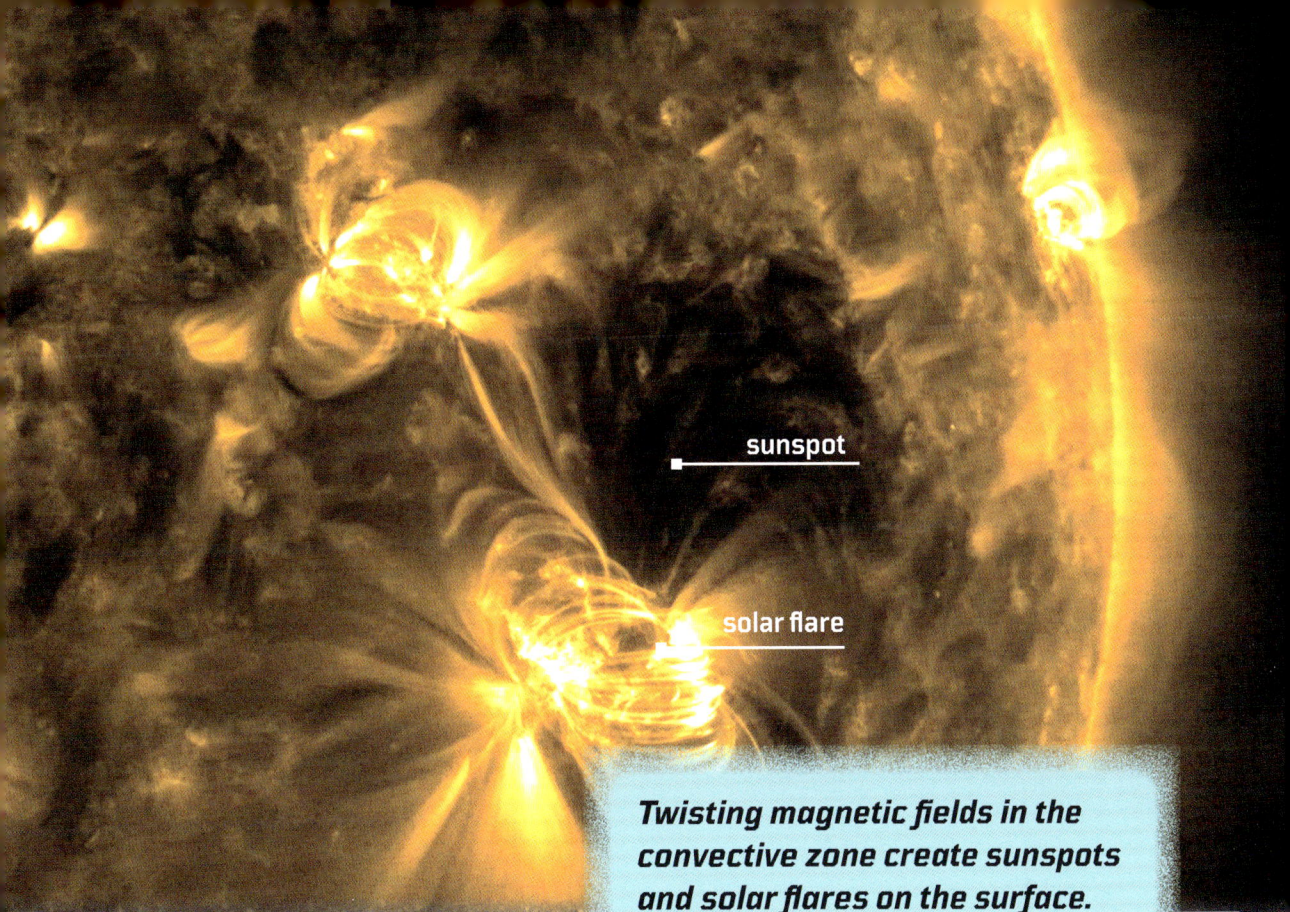

Twisting magnetic fields in the convective zone create sunspots and solar flares on the surface.

Convection is movement caused by heat. It occurs as hot material expands. It rises to the surface, where it cools and becomes denser. It sinks back toward the core, where it heats up and rises again. The temperature at the bottom of the Sun's convective zone is 360,000 °Fahrenheit (200,000 °C). Near the surface of the zone, it cools to 10,200 °Fahrenheit (5,650 °C).

Solar Magnetism

A simple magnet produces a magnetic field with two poles, north and south.

The Sun's magnetic field is far more complicated. Miniature magnetic fields called **flux tubes** rise through the convective zone to the Sun's surface. These magnetic flux tubes influence the appearance of the Sun's surface. The changes in the flux tubes cause dramatic sunspots and solar flares to appear on the Sun's surface.

The Sun's magnetic field is very unstable. About every 11 years, it flips so that magnetic north becomes magnetic south, and vice versa.

sunspot

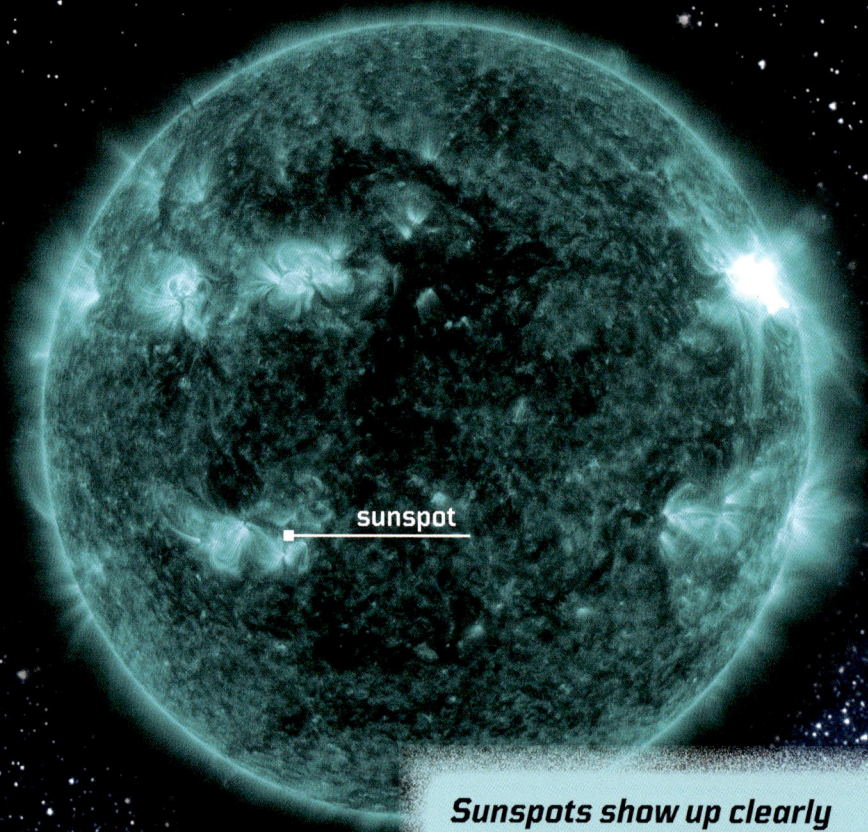

Sunspots show up clearly on images from X-ray and gamma-ray detectors.

At the Surface

The layer where light leaves the Sun and heads out into space is called the **photosphere**. It is sometimes described as the visible surface of the Sun, but in fact the photosphere is 62 miles (100 km) thick. Like the rest of the Sun, this outer shell is made up of gas and plasma.

Turbulent Surface

To the naked eye, the photosphere appears as a bright white disk. Looking at the Sun through a telescope reveals that the photosphere is not uniform. The Sun's magnetic field and convection currents can be seen at work on the surface. The magnetic field creates darker spots called sunspots, as well as brighter spots called faculae. Individual **granules**, or distinct particles, about 620 miles (1,000 km) wide move across the surface as hot fluid rises up from below. These granules move at up to 4.3 miles per second (6.9 km/s)

Like the Sun's interior layers, the photosphere is a violent place. Twisting magnetic fields push and carry the Sun's plasma. When these magnetic fields snap back, they can release huge amounts of energy. This can send giant solar flares rising off the photosphere and into the Sun's atmosphere.

Hot Atmosphere

The Sun's atmosphere is hotter than its surface. The temperature rises in a series of layers. Immediately above the photosphere is the **chromosphere**, which is heated to about 10 times the temperature of the surface. After a crossover region where the temperature increases rapidly in the space of just 62 miles (100 km), the next layer is the corona. This part of the Sun's atmosphere is made of plasma that has been heated to over 1.8 million °Fahrenheit (1 million °C). Scientists are still not sure why this happens. They guess that the Sun's magnetic field must be interacting with the plasma in the corona in some way that causes it to heat up.

Careful study has shown that the corona, like the photosphere, is not uniform. Streamers and **plumes** rise from the Sun's surface. Looping shapes called **coronal loops** arch around sunspots. They are shaped by magnetic field lines rising from the Sun's surface.

A series of solar flares light up the corona, which is usually darker than the photosphere.

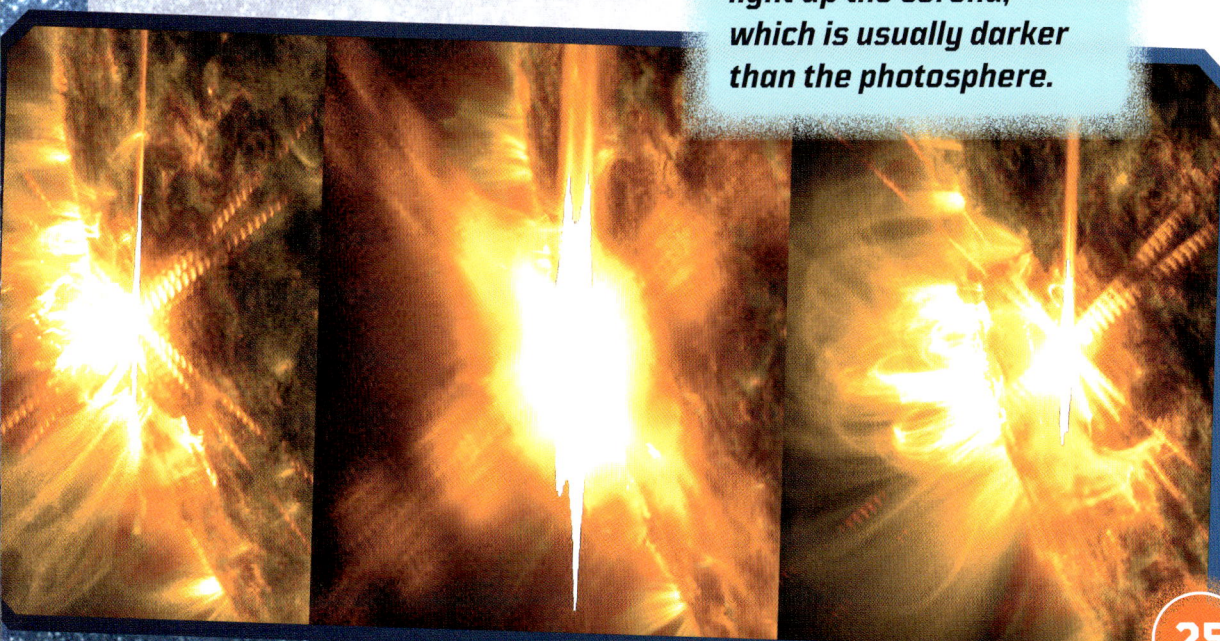

CHAPTER 4

Solar Power!

The Sun's **nuclear** furnace releases a huge amount of energy, which comes in a wide variety of different types. These include light, which is made up of photons, as well as ultraviolet and infrared radiation, X-rays, and gamma rays.

Light and Radiation

The higher the energy these particles carry, the more damage they can do. Ultraviolet radiation gives people sunburns and skin cancer, and can lead to blindness. However, it is also a good disinfectant and is used to clean tools and water. X-rays pass through soft tissues but are blocked by bones. Doctors use X-ray images to study broken bones and identify medical problems in patients. Too much X-ray exposure destroys **cells**, which are the smallest building blocks of living things. This exposure can kill. Gamma rays have the highest energy. They are a deadly form of radiation.

The Ghost Particle

The Sun also gives off **neutrinos**, which are tiny particles that help make up atoms. About 65 billion neutrinos pass through every square inch (6.5 sq cm) of Earth every second. People cannot see or feel neutrinos and they are also difficult for scientists to detect. That is why they are sometimes called ghost particles. Physicist Enrico Fermi named the particle the neutrino, which is Italian for "little neutral one."

X-rays have been used in medicine since their discovery in 1895. They can be captured by types of sensitive paper.

Scientists discovered the neutrino when they were exploring nuclear fusion inside the Sun. They realized their **equations**, or calculations, were not working. A lot of the mass and energy being released by the Sun could not be detected. Scientists wondered whether this missing material might be in a form that was too small and not energetic enough to find—the neutrino.

MISSION:
Space Science

In May 1999, the Sudbury Neutrino Observatory (SNO) began to look for neutrinos. The observatory was built 1.3 miles (2.1 km) underground in an old mine outside Sudbury, Canada, to shut out all other solar radiation. A large tank was built to contain heavy water. Heavy water is a special type of water **molecule** made up of an **oxygen** atom and three hydrogen atoms instead of the normal two. This makes the water denser, and better able to be hit by a passing neutrino. Detectors around the tank see a rare flash when a neutrino collides with a water molecule. The detector gave the first clear evidence that neutrinos existed and had mass. This greatly improved our understanding of the Sun.

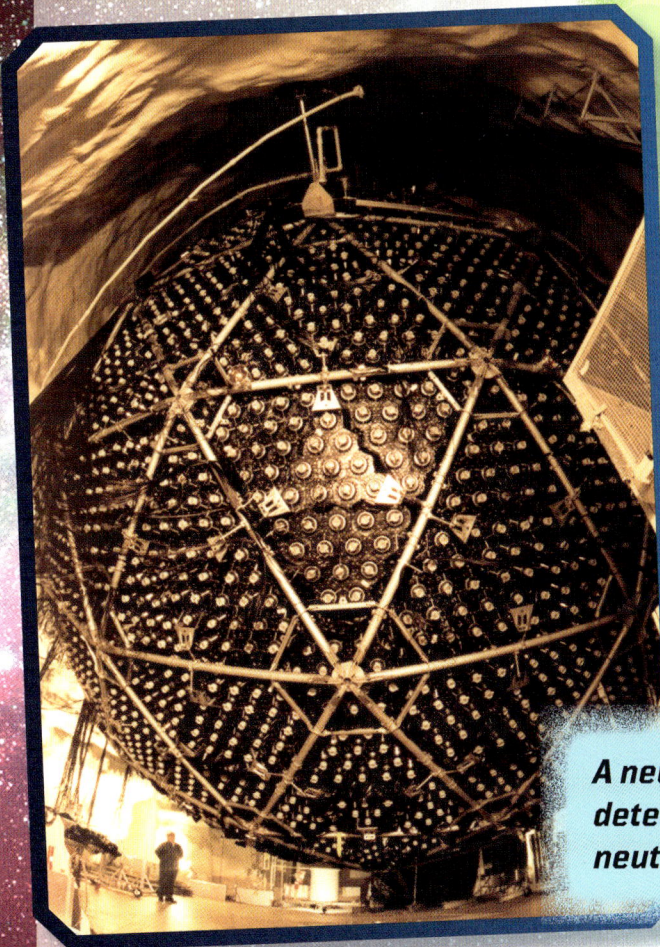

A neutrino detector tank has detectors to register flashes if a neutrino strikes a water molecule.

27

Solar Magnetism

Astronomers looking at the Sun detected dark areas on its surface which they called sunspots. Looking closer, they found that these areas were cooler than the rest of the Sun's surface. Pictures are altered to make sunspots appear dark, so they are visible. However, although they are darker than the rest of the Sun's surface, sunspots are still extremely bright. They are also temporary, only lasting up to a few months.

Sunspots usually form in groups and pairs of sunspots are magnetically the reverse of each other. Scientists suspect that sunspots form because of the Sun's magnetic fields. Some scientists believe that magnetic flux tubes created in the convective zone cool the surface down as they rise.

Solar Weather

The rate at which sunspots appear rises and falls over a period of about 11 years. This is the same as the period when the Sun's magnetic field reverses. The period when sunspots are most common is called **solar maximum**, and the period of lowest activity is called **solar minimum**.

Sunspots are 10–100,000 miles (16–161,000 km) across.

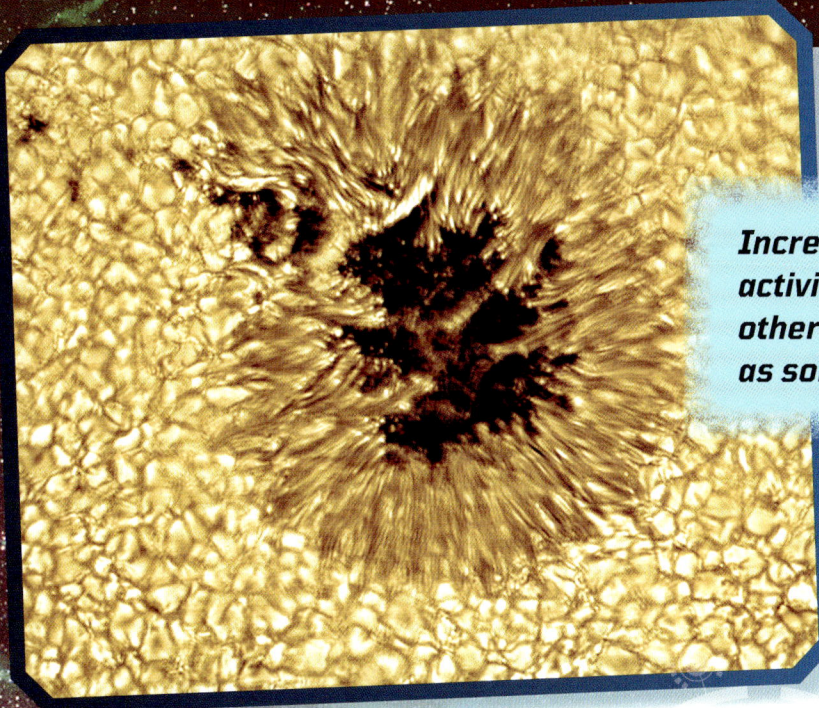

Although sunspots are dark, the area of the Sun around them gets brighter. This is because a sunspot keeps heat from rising from below. This heat increases and flows around the sunspot, brightening the surrounding area by more than the sunspot dims it. Some people wonder if sunspot activity influences **climate change** by making the Sun brighter. Climate change is the process by which Earth's global weather is changing. However, the role of sunspots is small compared to the changes caused by pollution and the **greenhouse effect**.

MISSION:
Space Science

Researchers at Stanford University have invented a way to to predict the appearance of sunspots. Just as detectors on Earth sense **seismic waves** from earthquakes, detectors on SOHO listen to the Sun. They can pick up the sound waves that precede the sunspots rising to the surface. Using this technique, scientists have detected sunspots before they appear. They hope to use this in the future as a means of forecasting solar weather.

Flaring Up

The photosphere and atmosphere of the Sun are violent places. Twisting magnetic fields form between the photosphere and the corona. They have enough energy to pull at parts of the Sun's plasma, pulling them at speeds close to the speed of light.

A coronal loop occurs when a magnetic flux tube rises from the photosphere into the corona. It pulls the Sun's plasma in an arch across thousands of miles of the surface. As the magnetic fields twist and snap, they build up energy like an elastic band being pulled to its limit. When the magnetic fields "snap," the energy of the flux tube is released. It creates an explosion on the Sun's surface that sends streams of plasma shooting out into space. This is called a solar flare.

Huge coronal loops are often linked to sunspots on the Sun's surface.

Invisible Blasts

Solar flares can be larger than Earth itself. Many solar flares contain energy at frequencies beyond visible light. This means that astronomers cannot see them through regular telescopes, although they can detect them using telescopes, or X-ray or gamma-ray detectors. These invisible flares carry huge numbers of **radioactive** particles and particles carrying electricity into space. The energy from a solar flare travels so quickly it can reach Earth in just eight minutes. Fortunately, Earth's magnetic field protects it and keeps the streaming flares from reaching its surface. However, the flares can still cause problems by disrupting radio waves and **satellites** in orbit.

Solar Cannonball

If a solar flare is like a gun firing into space, a CME is more like a cannonball. CMEs are massive bursts of charged particles fired into space. These can take up to three days to travel to Earth, and they hold their shape more than flares. CMEs have enough energy to push deep into Earth's magnetic field. The charged particles are channeled to Earth's magnetic poles, where they hit the atmosphere and make the particles of gas in the air glow. This produces a brilliant light display known as the *Aurora Borealis* or Northern Lights in the north and the *Aurora Australis* or Southern Lights in the south.

Large CMEs can cause problems with Earth's electrical systems. In 2006, NASA launched a new observatory called the Solar Terrestrial Relations Observatory (STEREO) to monitor CMEs.

YOUR MISSION

Why do you think it is so important to monitor CMEs? How might advance warning of CMEs be able to help people on Earth? How might a large solar flare affect our daily life on Earth?

The aurora takes place 50–400 miles (80 to 644 km) above Earth's surface.

Solar Wind, Planet Killer

The Sun is an explosion in space that has lasted for more than 4.6 billion years. It creates vast amounts of energy in the form of light, heat, and charged particles. The particles in the corona are heated to 1.8 million °Fahrenheit (1 million °C). They become so energized they can no longer be held back by the Sun's gravity. They stream away from the star as the solar wind, reaching speeds of up to 500 miles per second (805 km/s). Scientists first guessed the existence of the solar wind when they noticed that the "tails" of comets always pointed away from the Sun, whether they were approaching the Sun or moving away from it. The tail sometimes stretched ahead of the comet. Something was blowing the dust in the comets' tails away from the Sun.

The planets are constantly bombarded by the solar wind. It is powerful enough to damage living cells. Some planets, including Earth, have a magnetic field to protect them. This field deflects the charged particles, keeping them from reaching the planet's surface. The particles that are caught in Earth's magnetic field are drawn to the planet's magnetic poles, creating auroras.

The solar wind pushes against Earth's magnetic field, making it stretch out like a tail.

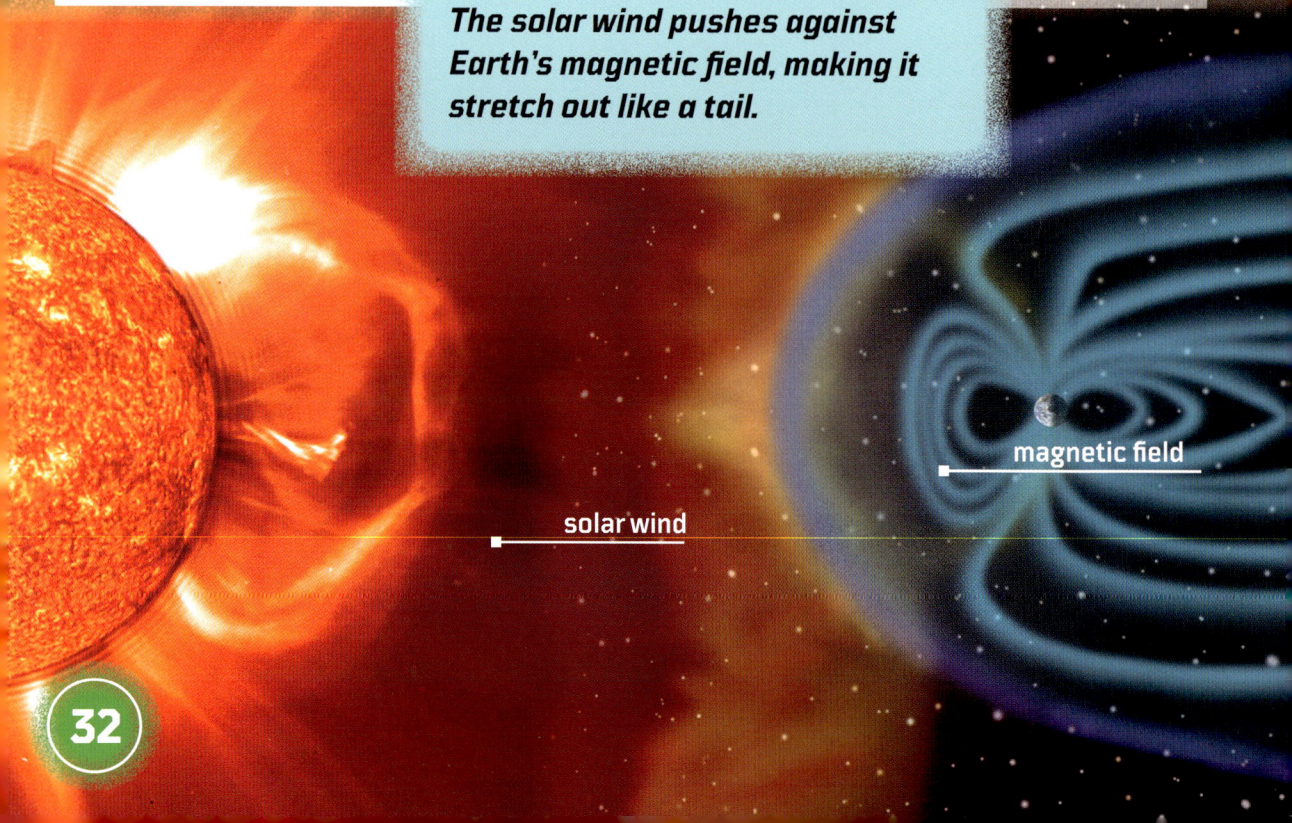

magnetic field

solar wind

In 2018, Voyager 1 detected changes in outside radiation that suggested it was passing into the heliopause.

Planets Without Protection

If planets lack a magnetic field, the solar wind beats at the atmosphere. Over millions of years, the solar wind can rip away a planet's atmosphere. Scientists think this happened to Mars. It used to be an ocean world, but is now dry and lifeless. The solar wind affects satellites in orbit, which have less protection from Earth's magnetic field. Satellites used for Global Positioning Systems (GPS) have been affected, disrupting navigation systems.

The solar wind extends beyond the planets and up to 100 to 120 AU into space. It stops at a limit known as the heliopause, which may be the farthest extent of our Solar System. Only one spacecraft, NASA's Voyager 1, has ever flown that far. In spite of the damage the solar wind does to planets such as Mars, it might also be helpful. The solar wind pushes against an area at the edge of our Solar System called the interstellar medium, keeping it away. This interstellar medium is radioactive and therefore damaging to life.

YOUR MISSION

If Earth's magnetic field was weakened, how do you think this might affect its atmosphere? How might this change our planet?

CHAPTER 5

Solar Danger

Between August 28 and September 2, 1859, astronomers observed a big increase in sunspot activity. The auroras at Earth's north and south poles became brighter. They could be observed as far north as Queensland, Australia, and as far south as the Caribbean Sea. Finally, on September 1, English astronomers Richard Carrington and Richard Hodgson spotted an enormous solar flare.

Solar Disaster

The flare was part of a very large CME. Taking just 17 hours 36 minutes to travel the distance from the Sun, the CME carried enough energy across space to Earth to power all of today's electrical appliances for 2 million years. Charged particles became caught in telegraph wires, which gave telegraph operators shocks, and caused the telegraph network to fail. Some operators were unable to send and receive messages—even after unplugging and reactivating their devices.

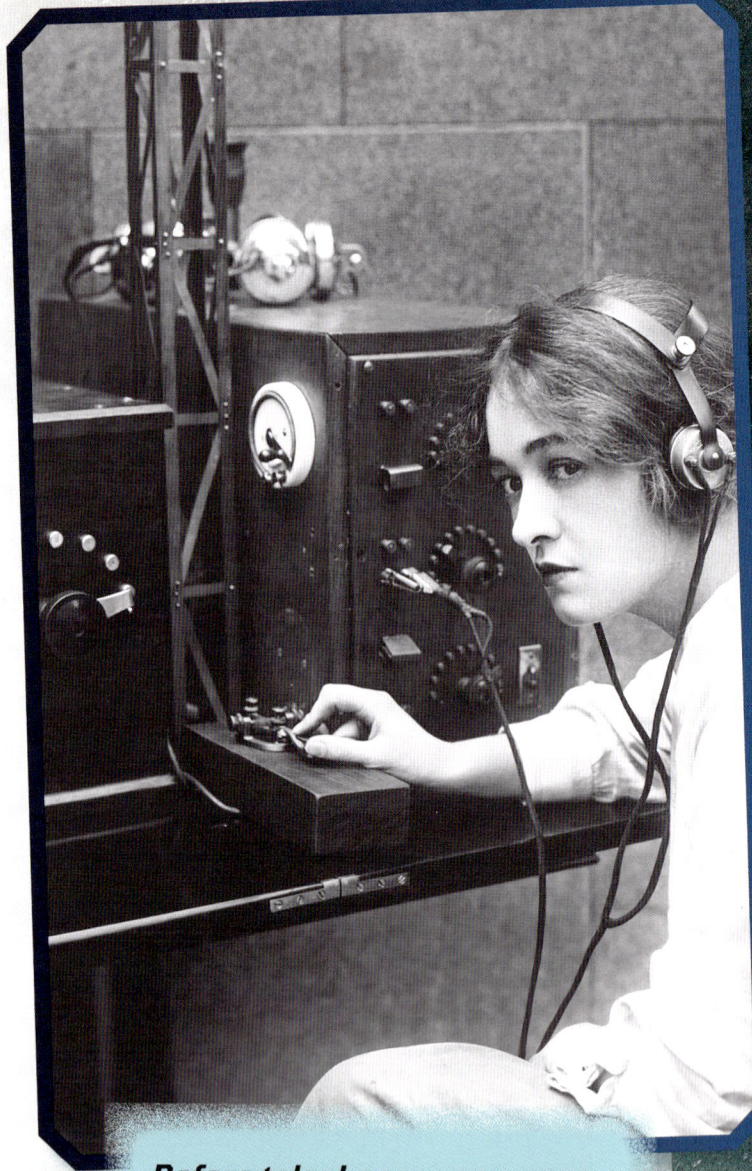

Before telephones, messages were sent by telegraph, which used radio signals to transmit a code of dots and dashes.

A Different World

The 1859 event is known as the Solar Superstorm. Had it occurred years earlier, no one might have noticed. The only sign would have been the impressive auroras, because the telegraph system was not yet invented. Had the superstorm occurred today, in contrast, the effects could have been disastrous. Today, power lines run for hundreds of thousands of miles across the land. Most houses have computers and appliances that could be damaged or destroyed by power surges caused by a CME. The power grid could collapse. Scientists estimate it could take up to ten years and cost trillions of dollars before Earth could fully recover. Being without power for a day is a minor inconvenience, but being out of power for months could disrupt food and water supplies that rely on electricity.

Disaster Waiting to Happen

Less severe CMEs have hit Earth since 1859. One in March 1989 knocked out power across large parts of Quebec, Canada. In July 2012, scientists observed a strong CME that missed Earth by just nine days. Scientists are looking for ways to limit the effects of CMEs. It may be possible to shield wires and electrical systems from charged particles, but there are so many appliances in existence that the task may be impossible. Scientists are also planning space missions to send probes far into space to spot CMEs as they approach. With enough warning, it might just be possible to turn off all the electricity on the planet, which could save Earth from a total loss of power that might last years.

Power lines can catch the charged particles of CMEs, creating power surges that can destroy equipment and shut down power stations.

Dangerous Defenders

Even when CMEs are not taking place, the Sun is spewing out charged particles all the time. Many of these particles are headed toward Earth. The planet's magnetic field helps protect it. So do two belts of radiation that extend from 310–36,000 miles (500–58,000 km) above Earth's surface. These are the inner and outer Van Allen radiation belts. They form when parts of the solar wind are captured and held by Earth's magnetic field. The gap between the inner and outer belts lies between 8,700–15,500 miles (14,000– 25,000 km) above Earth's surface. This is referred to as the "safe zone."

Recent Discovery

In the first half of the 1900s, some scientists began to suggest that these belts could exist. However, their existence was not confirmed until 1958, when the space probes Explorer 1 and Explorer 3 flew through them. Astrophysicist James Van Allen used measurements taken by devices on the probes to confirm that the radiation belts did indeed exist. As a result, the belts were named for him.

This illustration imagines the Van Allen belts that extend above Earth's surface, along with the Van Allen probes.

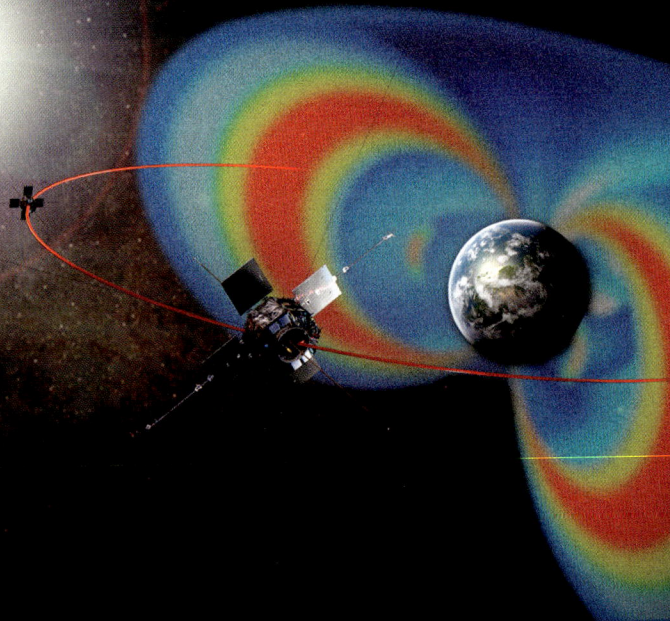

MISSION:

Space Science

Physicists including a Russian physicist named V.V. Danilov have proposed a way of draining the lower Van Allen Belt of its radiation, using a system of 62-mile-long (100-km) high-voltage wires to deflect the radioactive particles into outer space. They estimate they could eliminate the threat to satellites in low Earth orbit. While this would help protect satellites or astronauts flying through the belts, many scientists think it could be dangerous to tamper with one of Earth's shields against the solar wind.

James Van Allen launched instruments into space to measure radiation.

NASA Mission

In 2012, NASA launched the Van Allen Probes, which were designed to study the inner and outer radiation belts in more detail. Six years later, they were still in orbit. The probes discovered a third temporary belt of radiation that formed briefly within the "safe zone" between the inner and outer belts. After existing for a month, the radiation belt faded. It reappeared later, during a period in which the solar wind blew with more energy than normal.

The Van Allen radiation belts help deflect the solar wind and keep it from hitting Earth's atmosphere. This prevents the atmosphere from being slowly ripped off into space. However, the radiation from the Van Allen belts can damage satellites and can affect astronauts who are exposed to it for too long. Scientists planning future missions to the Moon or to Mars will have to keep the belts in mind as they plan their crafts' **trajectory**, or flight path, to minimize danger to the crews.

The Future of the Sun

When scientists figured out how the Sun was powered, they also realized that the star would not last forever. After burning for more than 4.6 billion years, the Sun is still 70 percent hydrogen. As it continues to fuse that hydrogen into helium, however, the Sun's core will eventually run out of hydrogen. This will happen about 5 billion years from now. The Sun will undergo great changes. As hydrogen fusion in the core stops, gravity will pull the material in the core tighter together. Heat and pressure will increase until helium atoms are fused into **carbon**.

Red Giant

The heat will also cause the Sun to start fusing the hydrogen around its core. This will cause its outer layers to expand. Between 5 to 7 billion years from now, the Sun will stop being a yellow dwarf and turn into a red giant. It will grow to 256 times its current size, swallowing the orbits of Mercury and Venus, and possibly Earth as well. Even if Earth escaped being swallowed, it would be uninhabitable. Long before the Sun's expansion, its higher temperatures will boil away the oceans and make life on the planet impossible.

From a yellow dwarf (top), the Sun is expanding into a red giant (bottom) so hot that life on Earth will be impossible.

White dwarfs are the burned-out cores of old stars.

White Dwarf

Our Sun is not large enough to fuse carbon and trigger a huge explosion called a **supernova**. Exploded stars sometimes become **black holes**. Instead, when it runs out of helium to fuse, it will release its outer layers, shedding half of its mass into our Solar System and creating a nebula. The core will remain, as a type of small, bright star called a white dwarf. White dwarfs take billions of years to cool. In fact, the universe has not existed for long enough for the first white dwarfs to have cooled down enough to lose their brightness.

YOUR MISSION

In 5 billion years' time, humans might be able to find a new place to live in our Solar System as the Sun becomes a red giant. Mars could heat up to the point where it could once again support complex life. The same could happen with Jupiter's moon Europa or Saturn's moons Titan and Enceladus. The heat from our giant Sun could even make it possible to live on Pluto—the dwarf planet far from the Sun. Where in our Solar System would you prefer to live? How might you **colonize** that place?

CHAPTER 6

What's Next?

For something we cannot live without, it is amazing how much no one knew about the Sun until the last 200 years. Since the earliest civilizations, most people have taken the Sun for granted. They assume it will rise every morning. However, some ancient Babylonians and Greeks, and later astronomers such as Edmond Halley and Isaac Newton, wanted to know more. Their observations helped scientists figure out the true nature of the Sun. They also revealed that there are many mysteries still to be solved.

Growing Understanding

Thanks to these scientists, we know that the Sun is a star. We know that hydrogen fuses in the Sun's core. We understand that this produces the light and heat that keep Earth alive. We also know that it produces other radiation, from infrared and ultraviolet light, to X-rays and gamma rays. We have even discovered neutrinos, particles so tiny they are invisible. We know that the Sun is unpredictable. We know that solar flares and CMEs can hit Earth, and we are starting to understand how dangerous this could be to all of us.

Some scientists think Stonehenge was built to measure the changing position of the Sun, because the stones line up with sunrise and sunset on the longest and shortest days of the year.

MISSION:

Space Science

New Tools for Research

New technologies will help us push the boundaries of what we know about the Sun. X-ray and gamma-ray detectors will give us more detailed pictures of the Sun. They will reveal details we have not yet been able to see.

Scientists listening to the vibrations or "sounds" the Sun makes are already predicting when sunspots will form. This could give us some early warning of an approaching CME. It might allow us to take steps and buy us enough time to protect vital electrical systems on Earth.

In 2009, NASA launched the Kepler Space Telescope to look for planets in other solar systems, including planets similar to Earth. It is also helping astronomers observe stars that are similar to our Sun. In 2012, NASA announced that the space telescope had mapped Kepler-30. This system, 10,000 light-years away, shows a star and planets orbiting in much the same way ours do. This suggests that systems of rocky planets orbiting a medium-sized star are common. It also shows that when they first form, they look much the same as the planets in our own Solar System looked when they were first created.

Big Questions

In spite of all we have learned about the Sun in the past few decades, many mysteries remain to be solved. Many scientists are dedicated to solving these mysteries, even as each new discovery seems to provoke more questions. One big question is why the Sun's corona is so much hotter than the surface of the Sun. In most cases, the farther you go away from a heat source, the colder you become. So what is supercharging the Sun's atmosphere? The solar wind itself is another mystery. Although we know what it is made of, scientists are not sure what forces push this wind away so fast. Then there is the question about why the Sun produces X-rays and gamma rays.

The Missing Neutrinos

While scientists have proven the existence of neutrinos, and helped answer questions about how the Sun works, one mystery about neutrinos remains. Based on what scientists have detected, they have found only one-third of the number of neutrinos that should exist. Where are the rest? The search for these ghosts continues.

The Sun provides power to satellites orbiting Earth, including the International Space Station (ISS).

NASA welcomes images of the Sun from amateur astronomers—but always observe the Sun safely!

Scientists are still figuring out how the Sun's magnetic field works, and why sunspots appear when they do. They ask why the Sun goes through periods of intense sunspot activity and other periods of calm. During the Maunder Minimum between 1645 and 1715, for example, only 50 sunspots were observed. Based on normal activity, there should have been more than 40,000. Scientists hope that a better understanding of sunspots will help them anticipate large solar activity.

Future Missions

Scientists and astronomers continue to search for answers, and new technologies will help. Bigger telescopes such as the Daniel K. Inouye Solar Telescope will provide important new data for scientists to study. New satellites and space probes will bring us closer to the Sun for answers. The unmanned Parker Space Probe will travel to within 3.7 million miles (6 million km) of the Sun's surface. NASA hopes that at this distance the space probe will be able to gather important information about the Sun that might help solve some of its mysteries.

We may always have questions about the Sun, but as long as scientists and astronomers continue to observe and investigate, we will continue to peel away the mysteries of the most important object in our Solar System.

Your Space Science Mission

In this book, you have read about how scientists have explored the mysteries surrounding the Sun. You have learned how they continue to increase their knowledge about Earth's star. You have discovered missions that have provided answers to some of the most important questions about our Sun. You have also learned about future planned missions to our Sun.

Now it's your turn to design a mission! Getting anywhere near the Sun is difficult and dangerous because of the extreme heat. For that reason, uncrewed probes are far safer than sending astronauts to study the Sun. How would you go about planning a mission to investigate the Sun? Here are some hints and tips to help get your space mission off the ground.

If you could design a craft to explore the Sun, what would it look like? Try drawing an image of how it might appear.

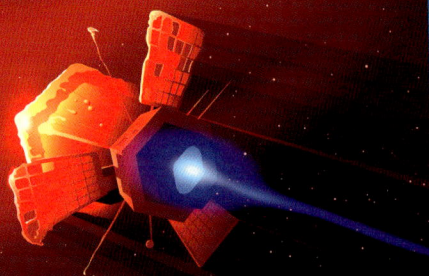

Planning Your Mission

1 Think about what you want to achieve or learn.

Do you want to find out more about the Sun's structure, or about the sunspot activity on its surface? Are you more interested in locating the Sun's missing neutrinos? Or perhaps you would like to find out more about how the star will change into a red giant.

2 Do your research.

Telescopes on Earth and in space have already provided detailed information about the Sun and the energy it gives out. Before you plan your mission, explore the work of some solar observatories to find out whether they have already begun to explore the areas in which you are interested.

3 Design your spacecraft.

How will it be powered? For the long journey to the Sun, solar sails or an ion engine might be best. Would it be possible to build a heat shield tough enough to protect a spacecraft from the heat of the Sun's corona?

4 Plan how you will gather information.

The Sun is too hot for anything to approach too closely, and it doesn't have a solid surface to land on. Your spacecraft will have to orbit the Sun while it studies the activity on the surface or tries to glimpse the interior.

5 Choose your instruments.

Think about the data you want to gather, and what tools would be best for the purpose. Most spacecraft carry cameras and spectrometers. What other devices might be useful?

6 Collaborate!

Once you have some ideas jotted down, share them with a friend. See if they can come up with suggestions and new ideas to add to yours.

Glossary

Please note: Some **bold-faced** words are defined where they appear in the book.

asteroids Small, rocky bodies that orbit the Sun

atoms The smallest units of an element

black holes Areas of space from which no light can escape

carbon A chemical element present in all living things

charged particles Tiny bits of electrically charged matter

chromosphere A layer in the atmosphere of a star

colonize To settle communities in a place

comets Bodies made of ice and dust that travel around the Sun

cosmic radiation Energy radiating from space

dense Closely compacted

dwarf planets Small bodies that orbit a star

electromagnetic energy Electrical or magnetic waves traveling in space

filters Screens that remove colors from light

gamma rays A type of electromagnetic radiation

gravity A force that attracts all objects toward one another

greenhouse effect The warming of Earth caused by heat in the atmosphere

heliospheric Related to the region around the Sun

helium A light, colorless gas

hydrogen A very light gas

infrared A type of invisible radiation

interact Act together

interstellar Related to the spaces between stars

lenses Pieces of glass used to concentrate light

light-years Units based on the distance light travels in a year

magnetic field A region with a magnetic charge

mass The amount of matter in an object

molecule A particle formed by atoms

night side The side of a planet that faces away from the Sun

nuclear Related to the center of an atom

nuclear fusion Forcing atoms to join together

oxygen A colorless gas

plumes Tall, thin shapes

poles The top and bottom of a planet or star

pollution Particles of dirt or dust in the air

probes Uncrewed spacecraft

radiation The emission of energy through waves or particles

radioactive Containing potentially destructive energy

satellites Natural or artificial objects that orbit a planet or star

seismic waves Energy from earthquakes

solar flares Bursts of high-energy radiation from the Sun's surface

solar observatories Observatories that monitor the Sun

solar system A group of planets that circles a star

sunspots Dark patches that appear on the Sun

telescopes Instruments that gather information about distant objects

ultraviolet An invisible form of energy

X-rays Invisible waves of electromagnetic energy

Learning More

Books

Bow, James. *Energy from the Sun: Solar Power* (Next Generation Energy). Crabtree Publishing Company, 2016.

Garbe, Suzanne. *The Science Behind Wonders of the Sun: Sun Dogs, Lunar Eclipses, and Green Flash* (The Science Behind Natural Phenomena). Raintree, 2016.

Green, Jen. *The Sun and Our Solar System* (Great Scientific Theories). Capstone, 2017.

Hawksett, David. *Our Sun: Can You Figure Out Its Mysteries?* (Be a Space Scientist!). PowerKids Press, 2018.

Hudak, Heather C. *The Sun* (Exploring Our Universe). ABDO Publishing, 2017.

Jefferis, David. *The Sun: Our Local Star.* Crabtree Publishing Company, 2008.

Websites

Find out what's happening with the latest space technology:
www.esa.int/esaKIDSen

Go here for quizzes and games that will test your knowledge of astronomy:
kidsastronomy.com

This NASA website has everything you need to know about our Solar System and NASA's space missions:
www.nasa.gov/kidsclub/index.html

Index

astronomers 5, 8, 9, 11, 12–13, 15, 16–17, 28, 30, 34, 40
astronomical unit (AU) 5, 18, 33
atmospheres 4, 6, 14, 25, 30, 33, 37
auroras 31, 32, 34, 35

black holes 39

chromosphere 25
climate change 29
comets 4, 9, 32
convective zone 22, 28
Copernicus, Nicolaus 12
core 20–21, 38, 39
corona 18, 25, 30, 32, 42
coronal loops 25, 30
coronal mass ejections (CMEs) 9, 19, 31, 34, 35, 40, 41

Earth 4, 6, 8, 9, 10, 14, 15, 19, 30, 31, 32, 34–35, 36, 37, 38
electromagnetic energy 22
electrons 21
energy 4, 6, 7, 8, 9, 10, 11, 12, 20, 21, 22, 25, 26, 27, 30, 31, 34
European Space Agency (ESA) 9, 19

flux tubes 23, 28, 30
formation of the Sun 10

galaxies 4, 6, 7, 11
Galilei, Galileo 12
gamma rays 12, 17, 19, 22, 26, 30, 41, 42

gravity 4, 6, 10, 12, 19, 20, 21, 38
green flashes 15

Halley, Edmond 15, 40
heliopause 33
helium 7, 10, 13, 16, 20, 21, 38, 39
Herschel, William 12, 13
hydrogen 7, 10, 11, 13, 16, 20, 21, 27, 38, 40

interstellar medium 6, 33

Kepler, Johannes 15
Kepler Space Telescope 41

Lagrange points 19

magnetic fields 6, 18, 23, 24, 25, 28, 30, 31, 32, 33, 36, 43
Mars 33, 39
Moon 12, 15

NASA 9, 18, 41, 43
neutrinos 26–27, 40, 42
Newton, Isaac 12, 13
nuclear fusion 10, 20, 21, 27

orbits 4, 6, 18

photons 22, 26
photosphere 24–25, 30
planets 4, 6, 12, 32, 33, 39, 41
plasma 21, 24, 25, 30
probes 18, 19, 35, 36, 37, 43, 44–45

radiation 6, 8, 12, 17, 26, 30, 33, 36–37, 40
radiative zone 22
Rayleigh scattering 14–15
red dwarfs 7
red giants 38

satellites 9, 30, 33, 37, 42, 43
Solar and Heliospheric Observatory (SOHO) 9, 29
solar eclipses 12, 15, 16
solar flares 8, 9, 16, 17, 18, 19, 23, 25, 30, 34, 40
solar nebula 10, 11, 39
solar observatories 9, 16, 17, 27, 31
Solar Superstorm 34–35
Solar System 4, 6, 10, 12, 33
solar wind 18, 19, 32–33, 36, 37, 42
sunspots 9, 16, 22, 23, 24, 28–29, 34, 41, 43

telescopes 9, 11, 12, 16, 17, 41, 43
temperatures 4, 20, 22, 23, 25, 32

Van Allen radiation belts 36–37

white dwarfs 39

X-rays 5, 8, 12, 17, 19, 22, 26, 30, 41, 42

yellow dwarfs 7, 38

About the Author
James Bow has written many books for children, from geography and science to history and topical debate. He has written a number of books about space science, which is one of his favorite topics.